Painless *Money* Talk

For Your Child and For You

"Why and How Some People Are Rich"

By

George N. Yamagata

All Rights Reserved. 2013 George N. Yamagata

ISBN-13:978-1493548163

ISBN-10: 1493548166

Disclaimer:

This publication is designed to provide competent and reliable information regarding the subject matter covered. However, it is sold with the understanding that the author and publisher are not engaged in rendering legal, financial or other professional advice. If legal or other expert assistance is required, the services of professionals should be sought. The author and publisher specifically disclaim any liability that is incurred from the use or application of the contents of this book.

Happy Anniversary, my dear

I love you

Introduction

This book is a result of our research about money.

We (my wife Natasha and I) wanted to teach our kids, Philip and Serina, how money works in this country, the United States of America. The question was, **"Why and how are some people rich?"**

I admit there was a self-serving reason. I thought, "If we figure it out, we will have a better chance to be rich too." The assumption was simple enough, yet it turned out to be correct.

We read a number of financial advice books and magazine articles, and browsed countless blogs over 14 years. We found so much great advice that has worked for many people and for us.

But these great ideas are scattered all over through many books and blogs, and are hard to find together.

In this book, we extracted the ideas from these books and blogs, and put them together. The information in this book is what we wished we knew when we were younger.

In the books and blogs, these ideas were buried in pages of letters. As a researcher I don't mind reading. But sometimes, seeing a large block of letters is pain. Besides, most of these great business books were not written for teens, my kids' age.

We wrote up the manuscript for our kids as we originally intended. Then we used the manuscript to teach our kids. So understand that this book is written mostly for the young who want to make a better life. The contents are valid for all age and Money level.

We kept it simple, so they can understand and use the knowledge. We say this book is more young-minded and/or right brain-friendly than regular books. In other words, it should be an easy read.

For this book to be truly useful, glancing through is not enough, though. For us, when ideas were presented in a very short and simple form, they had a surprising thought-provoking effect. They became Zen-like questions. We started thinking about them. We talked about what they meant.

I suggest you do the same. Translate and apply the contents to your own life. Then the knowledge will start working for you.

We also put suggestions for further learning in the lower right side of the pages and the end of the book. If you feel like it, go ahead and read them. They are suggested for a reason. Please understand that by the nature of our shortened idea presentation, there is no way we can fully translate the content of these books.

We are confident that we can now send off our kids with better information. If they use the information, it will become their knowledge and wisdom. They can be financially competitive in the future. The "American Dream" is changing. But it is still achievable.

Here we publish the book to share the information. This book would make a great gift. We hope this book is helpful for your child and for you.

George

Table of Contents

Greetings to the readers, who are living in this country, the capitalistic United States of America   19

The Game of Money in life   20

Chapter 1: What is Money?   21

Money is an important part of your wealth

You need Money to live in this society

We honor and trust Money

Money is a social reward for your service

Consumer/Critic vs Creator/Service provider

Money can buy many options

Time and Money

Money can help you to get whatever you want, good or bad

Emotion and Money

Money must circulate

Rich people and their Money make the world go round

Chapter 2: Your Attitude toward Money   33

Where are you? Where do you want to be?

They say Money is evil. Is it true?

Do I have to be smart to be rich?

You choose your path, and the path determines how much Money you can get

Do what makes sense to You

You get what you seek….Law of Attraction

Attract Money, do not chase it

Value is in the eye of the beholder

A cool head and discipline make you a better game player

The meaning of what you do and how you say it are significant

Rich people think alike

Chapter 3: Personal Finance 101   46

How Money flows (Remember This)

The money you have is a result of the balance of income and spending ("It's how much you keep that counts")

How do you keep more?

(3-1) Spending   50

Need vs Want

Frugal vs Making more money. Which wins?

Budgeting

Write it down

Check the Price tag

"Can I afford it?" "Show me the Money"

Housing (house payment/rent, gas, electricity)

Food

Clothing

Communication (TV, phone, internet connection)

Transportation (car, gas, bus, taxi, train etc)

Insurance (car, medical, dental, house).. Protecting what you have

Tax ..... Do not cheat. Manage and save.

Entertainment

Cause….Charity & Donation

(3-2) Income 66

Job/work income

Investment Return

Government welfare….don't depend on it

Multiple Streams of Income

On Saving ….Pay Yourself First (10% saving rule)

(3-3) Investment 72

Asset and Liability

Investment aims for Building/Buying Assets

Typical things people Invest

You choose your investment

Do not kill the Golden egg-laying Hen. Get more Golden egg-laying Hens instead

Do not put all eggs in one basket

You can be your own Biggest Asset (Education and Training)

Money can make more money

The Rich get Richer through Assets

You can retire when ….

(3-4) Stay away from Money Killers/Suckers   83

Medical bill. Stay healthy and be insured

High interest debt (Bad debt). Credit card and some loans

Bad habits

Divorcing and lawsuits

What if I don't/can't pay back?

Credit Score

Chapter 4: Family Finance   90

You are not alone when you have a family

You need to talk about Money in family

"People first, then money, then things"

Having and raising a child is expensive

Parents need to take care of themselves first

If parents don't teach kids about Money, who will?

Return of Investment for higher education

Chapter 5: How will You Make Money?   98

(5-1) Choosing Your ways to make Money

Your Life comes first. Choose your path wisely

Decide what you want

Have a Dream. Write it down.

Making Money is a Process

Don't just hope, make sure it happens

Learn your art to make it your trade

Meet the Real Deal

Solve problems

Do what you are good at

Do what counts

Right Attitude plus Specific knowledge

How do you choose what you do?

Research then Commitment

Track, path and pyramid

"What do you do for a living?"....Keep it simple

Good idea...can YOU do it?

Employer vs Employee

Risk

"Feel Fear and Do It Anyway"

Failure is an inevitable process of the game

Schools can give you a protected time to learn skills to make money

Personal branding..... "I am X and I do Y"

Don't be insane, but...

(5-2) Professionals 1: Employees   122

Virtue in the life of Service

An Employee can be expensive

Hiring people (employers) want to hire decent employees

Be prepared and be useful

Urgent vs Important

From Do It Yourself (DIY) to Teamwork

Life in a corporate culture

(5-3) Professionals 2: Employers (including Self-Employed) 130

Also the life of Service, in a different manner

Choosing your Niche

Building his own business (Entrepreneur)

The first Chip…. get your Capital Money

Business Model

Sink or Swim

Great power comes with great responsibility

Think in numbers

You need to work on your business

Does it Work?

Who/What is your Business?

Money is blood to your business

Can the business sustain itself?

Build a Business that (eventually) does not need you

When it works, Repeat it

Chapter 6: Go for the Big Money   147

Money is unlimited when you know how to tap it

Who are the Very Rich people?

What do they do? Five common characteristics of what Rich people do

Age has little to do with being Rich

Fame, publicity and being Rich

Rich people (tend to) deal only with other Rich people

Other People's Money

Bring something to the table

Think Win-Win

Becoming High Rollers in Casino

Size matters…..It's a different Game now

Chapter 7: Life Long Strategy for Money
161

    Be prepared to move on

    On Windfall (Lottery, Inheritance)

    Which quarter are you in?

    Strategy and Game plan

    Once you have Money

    There are important things other than Money

Chapter 8: Grain of Salt   168

Everyone speaks for himself

Conflict of Interests may not be mentioned

Who is speaking?

Be Educated. Continue learning and working on your Money

Further Learning Suggestions	174
Reader's Responses	179
About the Author	180

Greetings to the readers, who are living in this country: the capitalistic United States of America

We intended the contents of this book to be understood, discussed and practiced by the young (mid/high school) and up. Depending on how prepared you are or when you pick up this book, you can be younger or older.

For the young people:

Reading this book and using the knowledge will give you a head start and tremendous advantage when it comes to your Money.

For older folks (like us):

There is so much money advice we wish we knew when we were younger. But it is always better late than never. They helped us a lot. If you need a turnaround in your financial life, this book can help you.

We wish best of luck to all the readers.

The Game of Money in life

All kids come to this world without knowing the Game of Money

To play the game,

Watch what's going on,

Get the rules,

Study good players,

And play the game well.

Chapter 1: What is Money?

What do you really think Money is?

Money is an important part of your wealth

Your overall "Wealth" is a sum of various aspects of your life

Bring Balance to the various aspects

"Career and Life Path, Spiritual Growth and Self-Cultivation, Health and Family, Money and Abundance, Fame and Reputation, Love and Marriage, Creativity and Children, Helpful People, Blessings and Travel " (Chinese Feng Shui)

"Spouse, Family, Money, Work, Possession, Pleasure, Friend/Enemy, Church, Self" ("Centers", the source of our security, guidance, wisdom, and power)

Feng Shui Your Life (Jayme Barrett)
The Seven Habits of Highly Effective People (Stephen Covey)

You need money to live in this society

You do not live alone

Our life is supported by various services and products provided by other people

We pay for them with Money

Money makes it easier for us to exchange our services, products, or something of value

The Ten Day MBA 4th Ed. (Steven A. Silbiger)

We honor and trust Money

Money is like a promise

By itself Money is just paper, metal, or numbers

In history, other things like seashells, stones, bags of rice, ammunition, toothpaste and razors worked as Money

Money is an abstract, functional being

When we honor and trust Money, Money becomes valuable and means something to us

The Ultimate Suburban Survivalist Guide (Sean Brodrick)

Money is a social reward for your service

Other people give you Money when you serve them or provide something

Money is a reward

When you serve or provide more people, or serve exceptionally well or provide something of high value, you make bigger Money ("Impact Millions")

The Millionaire Fastlane (MJ DeMarco)
The Ten Day MBA 4th Ed. (Steven A. Silbiger)

Consumer/Critic vs Creator/Service provider

There are two types of people:

The Consumer/Critic and the Creator/Service provider

Consumers pay Money to receive a Service or Product

Critics say something about someone else's Service or Product

Neither produces something of high value

Creators and Service providers create something of value and give it to others

In return, they can get Money, the reward

There are many things you do that do not make Money

You have to be a Creator or Service provider to make Money

The $100 Startup (Chris Guillebeau)

Money can buy many options

Money can buy many products and services

When you have a lot of Money, you are not confined by limited options

You get sick and can see the best doctor in the world

You want to travel and can just go

You want to help others and can use your Money to help them

The Money you have can do a lot of things on your behalf

Many Rich people use their Money for unique experiences, services or products

They donate a lot of Money to charity causes, too

No BS marketing to the Affluent (Dan Kennedy)

Time and Money

Usually people work to make Money

It takes your Time to work

When you have a lot of Money, you don't have to work

Your Time is freed

You use the Time for something you feel meaningful

This is the freedom your Money can buy for you

The Millionaire Fastlane (MJ DeMarco)
Go It Alone (Bruce Judson)

Money can help you get what you want, good or bad

Money is like a Genie who can grant many of your wishes

The wish can be good or bad

Money is just an enabler, or enhancer, of what you desire

By itself Money is a neutral servant for you

If what you desire is bad,

With Money you can do great evil

If what you desire is good,

With Money you can do great good

How Rich People Think (Steve Siebold)

Emotion and Money

A lot of Money can give you sense of Power,

Because you can do or buy a lot of things with it

Having no Money can make you feel powerless,

Because your options will be limited

When you connect Power and Money,

You can get emotional about Money

When you are thinking about Money,

You are actually thinking about Power

Just like the above,

A lot of times,

It's not about Money

It's about something else (Power, Security, Values, Dreams)

Find what it is for you

The Good Fight (Les&Leslie Parrott)

Money must circulate

Money is not meant to be hoarded

Money is meant to be circulated and traveling the world

If you just stash your Money

It can be as useless as old newspaper in the attic

"Circulate" is not the same as spending freely and wasting

As the master of your Money

You want to be wise with how you use your Money

You are born Rich (Bob Proctor)

Rich people and their Money make the world go round

Money can help make things happen

There are a few people who control a lot of Money

A lot of Money can be a lot of Power

So they can also control other people and things

In America, the Richest 10% of people have 90% of all the Money

They can wage war

They can keep peace

It depends on how Money is used

Chapter 2: Your Attitude toward Money

What does your attitude toward Money have to do with the Money you will have?

Everything

You may have some clothes you are not comfortable wearing?

Some people feel uncomfortable with Money

If some people see Money as evil

They are unlikely to wish to have Money

They are not going to be Rich

It's just like that

Where are you? Where do you want to be?

Some people have a lot of Money (the Rich),

Other people have very little or no Money (the Poor),

Most people have an in-between amount of Money, not a lot, nor very little (Middle class)

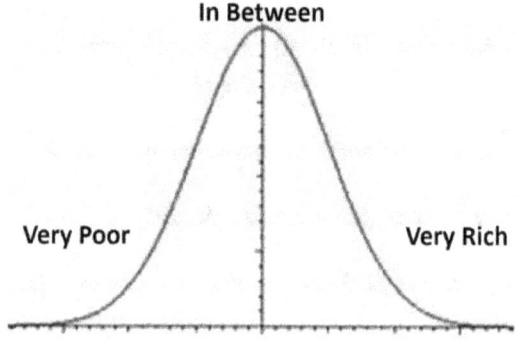

Where are you now?

Where do you want to be?

177 Mental Toughness Secrets of the World Class (Steve Siebold)

They say Money is evil. Is it true?

Yes and No.

Money only grants what YOU wish

When you are evil, your Money will do evil

Do I have to be smart to be Rich?

Being smart helps, but there are different types of smartness

School (academically) smart people are smart at reading, writing, remembering, and thinking-kind of things

They can be rich through specialized skills and high-paying work, like doctors or lawyers

Street smart people are smart at choosing what he can do to serve, and at creating where he can serve best

They can be business owners

With a successful business they can be very rich

You got to figure out what kind of smartness you have

You choose your path, and the path determines how much Money you can get

Not everyone has the type of smartness to be Very Rich

The best you can do is set your path according to what you got and what you can do best

Your likes and passions are important indicators for what you are made for

Remember,

You don't choose passion. Passion chooses you.

Or, when you become good at your art, it becomes your passion

What you do, and what value others find for it, determines how much Money you can get

Do what makes sense to you

You can try something that you are not made for

But it is not going to last for a long time

Psychologists say there are 16 different types of personalities

Each type of personality has strengths and weaknesses

It makes sense to do what matches your personality, who you are

Do What You Are: Discover the Perfect Career for You Through the Secrets of Personality Type
(Paul D. Tieger, Barbara Barron-Tieger)
I Could Do Anything If I Only Knew What It Was
(Barbara Sher, Barbara Smith)
Making a Living Without a Job, revised edition
(Barbara Winter)

You get what you seek....Law of Attraction

You will find what you seek with all your heart

Accordingly,

You seek Money and you will find Money,

when you seek Money with all your heart

However,

Since Money is a social reward, you need to seek Money by seeking what you can give to others, with all your heart

You do not seek Money itself

You seek what you can do best to others

Jeremiah 29:13 (Bible)
Law of Attraction (Michael Losier)
The Secret (Rhonda Byrne)

Attract Money, do not chase it

Do not chase Money by saying "I want to be Rich"

Instead, say "I am Rich because I do this"

Then choose what you do; Do something that you can do best, and that others find valuable

That something will attract Money for you and make you Rich

Envision that you are already Rich, then envision what you do

No BS Wealth Attraction in the New Economy
(Dan Kennedy)

Value is in the eye of the beholder

You create or provide something

But it is they who decide whether it is valuable to them or not

Since their needs/wants vary, you cannot sell your creation to everybody

You have to have your "Target" customer in mind

But consider they don't know what they want until it is presented

You can appeal to them through advertisement and persuasion

But eventually it is they who decide to buy

Van Gogh and Mozart died poor

Creating something of great value alone is not enough

Others with Money have to recognize it for you to make Money

Cashvertising (Drew Eric Whitman)
Tested Advertising Methods (John Caples)
Ogilvy on Advertising (David Ogilvy)

A cool head and discipline make you a better game player

Having a Hothead and lack of discipline is a surefire way to lose a game

In the game, situation changes

Only the combination of a cool head and discipline gives you a better chance in the changing situation

It is between You and Money

When it comes to Money

At least in the beginning of your Wealth creation

It is between You and Money

Do not care about Others

Only mind how You are doing with your Money

Consider only what is done or left undone by you

Trying to keep up with Others

Trying to show off your Money

Both are vain

When you make it, help others

Buddhist proverb
The Seven Habits of Highly Efficient People (Stephen Covey)
You were born Rich (Bob Proctor)

The meaning of what you do and how you say it are significant

You can lay bricks

Or you can build a Cathedral

You can dig a hole in a rocky land

Or you can help an African village to have a well

You may be doing the same thing

But which way of saying do you think is more meaningful?

See what you do in a different, meaningful way

You'll do best what is meaningful to you

The Success Principles (Jack Canfield)

Rich people think alike

Rich people make their Money in very different ways and in different industries

But the way they think and how they do things have common traits

If you want to be Rich, Study them, Think like they do,

and Act like they do

How Rich People Think (Steve Siebold)
177 mental toughness secrets of the world class (Steve Siebold)
Secrets of the Millionaire Mind (T. Harv Eker)

Chapter 3: Personal Finance 101

The relationship between you and your Money starts small, from personal finance, then grows to family finance and/or to Business finance

Learn the basics first

How Money flows (Remember This)

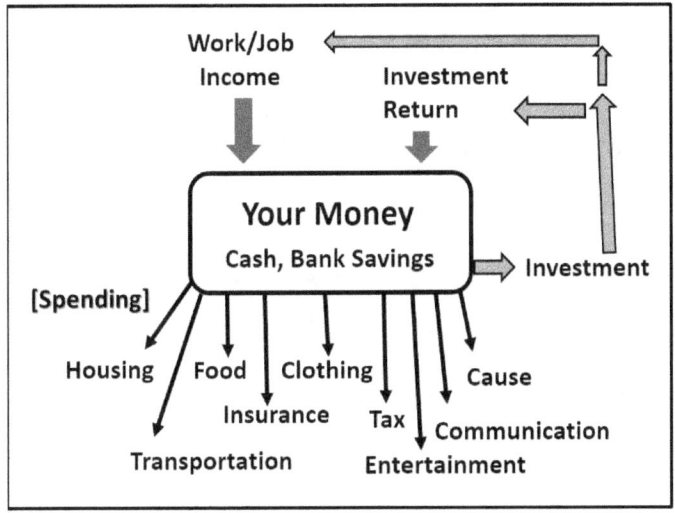

Overall Money flows like this

You have Money coming in through your Work/Job's income and your Investment Returns

You have Spending, for which Money is going out and not coming back

And You have an Investment, a special type of Spending

Your Money is going out and (may be) coming back bigger as your Investment Return

The money you have is a result of the balance of income and spending ("It's how much you keep that counts")

To be Rich, you want to increase the Money you have, or to have control over more Money

You can make a lot of Money

But if you spend as much as you make, you keep nothing

You are broke

Money is like water

You have a Dam

You have an upstream River (Money coming in)

You have a Downstream River (Money going out)

To keep more water in the Dam

What should you do?

How do you keep more?

It's simple

Make more

Save for yourself

Invest

Spend less

You want to think about how you are doing in these four tasks

(3-1) Spending

Spending is the Money going out from You and not coming back

Keep your Spending Smaller than what you make

Being a spendthrift, or being frugal, is going to help you keep more Money

Need vs Want

There are needs

That you cannot live without

There are wants

That you can live without

Some people mix up needs and wants

Know the difference between your needs and wants

Be prepared to cut down on the wants

Because wants are where you can waste your Money

Frugal vs Making more money

Which wins?

Being Frugal can cut down spending

You cannot cut your Spending to zero

Making can be limitless

You can make more Money than you can ever spend

Making more Money wins

Being Frugal is important

It shows your discipline

But if you want to be Very Rich

Focus on Making more Money

Focus on how you provide something of value to others

Budgeting

You are going to spend Money to live

You are going to decide how much Money is going to be spent, to which of these Spending categories

This allocation of your Spending is called Budgeting

Your Budgeting can tell you and others

What kind of spending is more important to you

Write it down

When you spend Money, write it down on paper

How much Money did you spend?

What did you spend the Money for?

At the end of the month, take a look at the paper

You'll know how much and on what you spent your Money

"Remember kids, the only difference between Science and screwing around is writing it down" (Mythbusters)

Writing it down is the first step to look at your Money like a Scientist does

Mythbusters (TV show)

Check the Price tag

When you buy something,

Check the Price tag

Is it the right price?

Does the something have the value as it says?

"Can I afford it?"
"Show me the Money"

Whether you can buy something or not is a matter of your Money

YOUR Money. Not someone else's. YOURS.

Show your Money to prove you have it before buying

You cannot buy it when you do not have the Money

Make Money first before you spend

Even if you have some Money, if your spending is not balanced, Probably it is your best interest not to spend the Money for "it"

The Suze Orman Show (TV show)

Housing (house payment/rent, gas, electricity)

You want to have a roof above you

You want to have a safe and comfortable place to sleep

You want a place to live in

A house or an apartment

With gas, electricity and water

All these cost Money

A house is usually one of the biggest expenses

It is better to be careful about the cost of housing

Home Buying for Dummies (Eric Tyson, Ray Brown)
The Money Book for the Young, Fabulous and Broke
(Suze Orman)

Food

Your Body is the vehicle that carries you through your life

You want to take good care of your Body

Eating is an important part of taking care of your Body

Some food work like medicine

You have to eat well

You can eat in many ways

Some eating options cost you more

Spending more on eating does not necessarily mean

You are eating well

Eating easily becomes your habit

You want to check whether your habit is a good one or not

The Real Age Diet (Michael Roizen, John La Puma)
The Green Pharmacy Guide to Healing Foods (James Duke)

Clothing

How you dress is an important indicator of

Who you are

You never have second chance to make a first impression

Good clothes open all doors

The Sartorialist (Scott Schuman)
Gentleman's Guide to Grooming and Style (Bernhard Roetzel)
Details Men's Style Manual (Daniel Peres)
The Pocket Stylist (Kendall Farr)
The Devil wears Prada (movie)

Communication (TV, phone, internet connection)

TV, phone, internet connection, Video games

It is easy to spend a lot of time on these

They can be addictive

Time spent on these can rob you of time creating something

Time spent on these likely puts you on the consumer's side

What if they are gone?

Are you going to use the time for something creative?

Or, are you going to find an equivalent to entertain yourself?

The Ultimate Suburban Survivalist Guide (Sean Brodrick)

Transportation (car, gas, train, taxi, bus etc)

For many people, the Car is the second biggest Spending next to the House

To some, their choice of car is connected to their Ego

To others, a car is a means to go from point A to B

There are many different meanings and standards for choosing

Big Spending moves big Money, so be extra cautious

Do your research

Keeping your car in good shape by taking good care of it can save Money in the long run

Learn how to do basic car maintenance

Auto Repair for Dummies (Deanna Sclar)

Insurance (car, medical, dental, house).. Protecting what you have

You may have a lot of things already and enjoy health

But they can be gone in a misfortune

A Fire, Flood, Earthquake, Tornado, Hurricane

Car accident, Sickness, Injury, Death, etc

Insurance is a system for which you pay some Money regularly,

Your Insurance company pools the Money from many people,

And pays the Money to the person who got struck by a misfortune

Car insurance pays for car damage and injury, and medical insurance pays for sickness and injury, for example

If no misfortune occurs to you, your Money is just gone

But it is good for you

In addition, Insurance can be used for savings and other purposes. Study how.

Tax ….. Do not cheat. Manage and save.

Tax Money goes to the Government, National and Local,

In the US, Income Tax return filing day falls on April 15th

They use the Taxpayer's Money for

Healthcare, Education, the Military, Infrastructure, Welfare, and many other things

The Governments need the Tax Money to function

They can Tax on all the Money that flows

On Income, Spending and Investment

The Rich with more Money get taxed more

There are specific ways to save on Tax

Like not paying unnecessary Tax by knowing the rules

Tax management is important for the Rich

Entertainment

"All work and no play make Jack a dull boy"

You want to be entertained sometimes,

There are many kinds of entertainments

And most entertainments cost you Money

Then they are a Spending

If you ask someone else to entertain you,

It's a service, you are a consumer, and you pay Money for it

If you entertain yourself,

By hobby or even by work, it's free for you

If you entertain others,

It can be a trade, your Business

And you can make Money from it

Yet you can still be entertained

Cause....Charity & Donation

There are good Causes

Like Curing Cancer or Helping the Poor

There are many groups and organizations for these causes

They also need Money to function and to survive

Many Christian Churches ask for tithing,

Donating 10% of the Money you make

The Cancer Research foundation throws a Fundraising Party

So they can fund research for cure

This is Spending,

But holds a special meaning to the person who is doing it

You can buy more satisfaction and blessings through this spending

Some Charity and Donation Money are Tax free, or can be used for reducing your Tax, too

(3-2) Income

How much Money you make is the key to being Rich

Job/Work income

Many adults have a job or some work

They provide a special service to get the job done

In return they get Money

If the service requires a high level of skill and training

They tend to get more Money for it

One way to be Rich is to have these high-paying jobs,

Work for long hours and many years

Live with discipline and accumulate Money over time

They get paid by the hour or by the job

If you want to be Rich through work

You need to work longer, do more work,

Or create something of very high value

The Millionaire Fastlane (MJ DeMarco)

Investment Return

Investments can take many forms

Investments can give you Returns

Returns can take many forms, like trust, a reputation and friendship

Some come back as Money

A return could be interest Money from Bonds you bought

A Return could be rent Money from the Apartment you landlord

A Return could be royalty Money from the book you wrote

The Good thing about an Investment Return is that it requires little or no further work from you

An Investment can be independent from you and can work while you sleep

Government welfare….don't depend on it

When you meet some requirements, like being Poor or disabled

The Government may give you Money, using other Taxpayer's Money

It's called Welfare

This welfare system was meant to be a temporal aid for unfortunate people to help them get back on their feet

Don't depend on it

By depending on something, you lose control over your own Money situation

That is a terrible condition

If the Government says that it cannot pay the Money any more,

What are you going to do?

Always aim to be independent, to be able to support yourself

Multiple Streams of Income

If you depend only on a single source of income

You are in trouble when the source dries out

Workers are unhappy when they lose their job, their only source of income

If you have multiple sources of Income

You are safer

Develop more than one source of Income

Have multiple streams of Income

Multiple Streams of Income (Robert G. Allen)

On Saving ....Pay Yourself First (10% saving rule)

When you make Money

Before you spend Money for anyone else, or for any one of the Spending categories,

Pay yourself first

Take away 10% of what you made

And save (invest) for yourself

The Money you saved can be for your Emergencies

The Money you invested can return bigger later

Make the saving automatic

The Richest Man in Babylon (George S. Clason)
The Millionaire Next Door (Thomas Stanley, William Danko)

(3-3) Investment

Investment is the key to being Rich or Very Rich

Remember the Money flow chart on page 47?

Even if you have one of the high-paying jobs

Or even if you have two or more jobs

What you can make by yourself (Job/Work Income) is limited

Because you have only limited time (24 hours/day), and you can do so much by yourself

That means, to be Rich fast or Very Rich,

You have to increase your Investment Return

Investment can take many forms

Choosing the right one for you is the trickiest part

Asset and Liability

Asset is something that puts Money in your Pocket

A Liability takes Money away from your Pocket

Rich Dad Poor Dad (Robert Kiyosaki)

Investment aims for Building/Buying Assets

When you use your Time and/or Money to build or buy something that you think would put Money in your Pocket (Assets),

It is called your Investment

Investment is Spending at first

Any Investment can make a big return or go sour

When it makes Money, it is an Asset; if not, a Liability

Risks for loss are inseparable from Investments

Investments are NOT Gambling

The difference is your knowledge and understanding

In an Investment, you know what you are doing and take a calculated Risk

In Gambling, you wish for the best with little knowledge and leave it to chance

Typical things people Invest in

Self (Training, Education)

People (family, friend)

Paper Assets (Bonds, Stocks, Mutual funds)

Real Estate (A House, Apartment)

Precious Metals (Gold, Silver, Platinum, etc)

Commodities

Currency

Rare Items

Other people's Businesses

Their own Business

Intellectual Property (book, patent, licensing)

You choose your investment

There are many Investments

Choosing is the tricky part

Do your research

Know Yourself

"Don't Buy What You Don't Understand"

The Essays of Warren Buffett: Lessons for Corporate America
(Warren Buffet, Laurence Cunningham)

Do not kill the Golden egg-laying Hen. Get more Golden egg-laying Hens instead

You know the story about the Golden egg-laying Hen:

"A Farmer and his wife had a Hen that laid a golden egg every day. They supposed that the Hen must contain a great lump of gold in its inside, and in order to get the gold they killed it. Having done so, they found to their surprise that the Hen differed in no respect from their other hens. The foolish pair, thus hoping to become rich all at once, deprived themselves of the gain of which they were assured day by day"

The Golden egg-laying Hen is your Investment

You kill it, and you will lose all income streams from it

Get more Golden egg-laying Hens

Aesop's Fables

Do not put all your eggs in one basket

When you put all your eggs in one basket

They all can be lost with one drop of the basket

If you put your eggs in different baskets

Even when a basket is dropped and the eggs are lost

You will still have some eggs in other baskets

"Putting eggs in different baskets"

It is called Diversification

It is a way to make sure you still have something

Even when a misfortune strikes

Diversification is important for your investment

You can be your own Biggest Asset (Education and Training)

Investment can come in many forms

Money you spend for your own education and training can increase your skills and ability to serve others

That can increase your own value

That can help you make more Money

Most Rich people believe in constant Education, Training and Improvement

Invest in yourself first

177 Mental Toughness Secrets of the World Class
(Steve Siebold)

Money can make more money

When you have a lot of Money

The Money can make more Money through interest for savings and Investment returns

Money is an Asset

"It takes Money to make Money" is true, at least in part

Don't be confused

Money is not the only thing that makes Money

Your service and/or assets are what makes your Money

The Question is,

How do you make the amount of Money that is enough to keep growing by itself

The Rich get Richer through Assets

When you have many Assets

They will keep returning Money to you

This is the simple mechanism

How the Rich get Richer

It doesn't matter whether he is a good person or not

He has more Assets that make him Richer

That is all

Rich Dad Poor Dad (Robert Kiyosaki)

You can retire when ....

You don't have to be old to retire

Poor people cannot retire even when they are old

Because they don't have enough Money to support their lives

When your non-Job/Work income reaches a sufficient amount to support all your Spending and your lifestyle,

Or, when you have the amount of Money sufficient to support you and your family for the rest of your life,

You can retire from your Job/Work

When Job/Work Income is not essential,

When the flow of Money is balanced and sufficient to support you and your life,

You have an option to retire (=live without a job)

(3-4) Stay away from Money Killers/Suckers

There are Money Killers/Suckers that rob you

Avoid them

Medical bills
Stay healthy and be insured

Everyone can get sick or injured

You would have to go to a hospital and see a doctor

And Medical care can cost you a lot

Stay healthy and injury free

Don't smoke

Don't drink too much

Eat well

Do modest exercise

Avoid being reckless

In case you get sick,

Be insured

High interest debt (Bad debt)
Credit card and some loans

They kindly lend you Money

In return, they want you to be their cash cow

You have to repay much more Money than you borrowed

(Original amount plus high interest)

Debts are not always bad. They can be used for leverage

But these debts are bad

Keep bad debt to a minimum

Pay it off as fast as you can

The Money Book for Young, Fabulous and Broke
(Suze Orman)

Bad habits

There are many things you buy out of habit

Even if it is not illegal drugs (which are devastating),

They can rob you of a lot of Money in the long run

A packet of cigarettes

Gourmet coffee in the morning

Eating out in a restaurant

They can add up quickly when you have them as habits

Bad habits are the opposite of good discipline

Money likes good discipline and comes to someone who has it

Money does not like bad habits and someone who has them

Money leaves consumers and goes to creators

Divorcing and lawsuits

When a family breaks apart, it splits the family Money

Divorcing is a Money killer

Even if you are good, there may be someone who wants to sue you. Legal issues have to be taken care of, often with lawyers with fees

Emotionally, it's draining

Time will be required, too

Get a prenuptial agreement and sign it before your marriage

You didn't lose anything if you didn't have to use it

And, have a lawyer friend

What if I don't/can't pay it back?

Sometimes you borrow Money

Borrowing is not always a bad thing

You can use more Money than you have by yourself

Using more Money is called Leverage

But when you end up with not paying back the Money you borrowed, it's not good, morally and practically

Your conscience may be nagging, for you broke their trust

Practically, they will come after you to pay it back

Then they will not want to lend you Money any more

So you cannot borrow any more

Even if they still lend you Money

They will charge higher interest

Do your best to pay back the Money you borrowed

Credit Score

Like an exam score in a class,

The financial industry developed a scoring system for your Money situation

That's called a Credit Score

If your score is low

They think you are untrustworthy or high risk

And will be reluctant to lend you Money

They don't want to lose their Money

If they think you are not going to pay back their Money

They will be reluctant

It would be irresponsible of them to lend their Money to someone who is unlikely to return it

Remain trustworthy

Trust, or Credit, is important for You

Chapter 4: Family Finance

You may be depending on your parents

You may be by yourself

You may have a family to support

All of you have to deal with Money

You are not alone when you have a family

When you have a family,

You have more responsibility

Maybe you have to provide for the family

Maybe you have to learn to be responsible about Money

Your attitude toward Money tends to be passed down in the family

Now it's a team sport

Each family member should learn how to play the Game of Money and play his/her role

You need to talk about money in family

Money is an important aspect in life

Like other moral and life skills,

Money skills should be talked about and taught in the family

Rich people do it

Many poor people don't

For the poor people,

It's a big handicap in the Game of Money

"People first, then money, then things"

Money is a servant to people

Not the other way around

When you reverse it,

People become a servant to Money

It's terrible

The Suze Orman Show (TV show)
You were born Rich (Bob Proctor)

Having and Raising a child is expensive

Having a child is a blessing

Raising a child takes responsibility

And a lot of Money

It takes planning and determination to have and raise a child

"It takes a village to raise a child"

(An African proverb)

A lot of support from and outside of the family helps to raise a child

Hopefully, the child grows wise enough to know this soon

Parents need to take care of themselves first

A parent has to be able to support themselves when they are old

No one will support his/her old age and retirement but themselves

Education for the young is considered an investment by society

Many organizations, groups and the government offer financial aid for the young

A parent has to aim to support their future self first,

Then aid the child

The Suze Orman Show (TV show)

If parents don't teach kids about money,

Who will?

Education about Money is important

Money skills are perhaps one of the most important life skills

Yet schools do not always teach it

Even if they teach, how can you be sure it is good teaching?

Take responsibility for learning and teaching about Money

In teaching and learning, follow advice from the good and skilled ones

Rich dad poor dad (Robert Kiyosaki)

Return of Investment for higher education

Higher Education (college and up) has become expensive

Calculate how much Money you are going to spend for college in 4 years

Calculate how much return you will get,

Like the first year's salary for the job you want to take after college

Does the cost-return make sense?

If it does not make sense,

Reconsider your plan for college and future Job/Work

Chapter 5: How will You Make Money?

(5-1) Choosing your ways to make Money

You choose your method of making Money and playing the Game of Money in your life

It's not about Money, It's about your choice

Money is only a result of your choice

In choosing, you have to consider who you are very carefully

And seek the best way you can serve to others

Then Money follows what you do

Your Life comes first. Choose your path wisely

What do you want from Your Life?

Your "want" is a powerful driving force for you

If you focus on making Money and neglect your life,

You may have Money,

But you may lose what is important to you

Consider what you are good at

What you are made for

Then choose your path

The amount of Money you would get should not be the single determinant of your life path

Decide what you want

Life is like a strange restaurant

You can have as much of whatever you want

But you have to place your order to get it

If you are not asking for anything and just sitting at the table

What is served may be different from what you really want

When you have what you want in your mind, you can place an order

Meaning that you can work toward it

Eventually life will serve it to you

How you see yourself in your mind, including how Rich you are,

is an important detail in your order

You are born Rich (Bob Proctor)
The Success Principles (Jack Canfield)

Have a Dream. Write it down.

"I have a Dream...."

You can be Very Rich when your Dream impacts millions and changes their way of life for the better

When your Dream is only about yourself,

You are likely the only one who cares about it

And Money will not come

Dream Big

Dream for the greater good

The Magic of Thinking Big (David Schwartz)
Thoughts are Things (Napoleon Hill)

Making Money is a Process

"A process" is something that happens over time

Dreams, Thinking, Ideas, Prayer,

They are all only in your head at first

You have to do something to make them happen

And that's the hard part

Doing something takes time, effort and education

And it is a process

It's like planting a seed and taking care of it

Without a seed, nothing grows

But if you don't take care of the seed,

It's likely to die before bearing the fruit

Do More Great Work (Michael Bungay Stainer, et al.)
Making Ideas Happen (Scott Belsky)

Don't just hope, Make sure it happens

If you know what you want to do, or have a dream, or have an idea, or what you hope,

Don't stop there. Make it happen

God helps those who help themselves

If you don't know how to make it happen,

Ask until you get an answer

Do not listen to the reason why or how you cannot

Ask how you can

Most things have been done before, and someone knows the answer. Find the person and ask how to do it well

If it has never been done, you have to come up with the answer

And do it yourself

The Aladdin Factor (Jack Canfield, Mark Victor Hansen)

Learn your art to make it your trade

Nobody is good at anything at first

You have to go through learning and training process to be good at anything

Be a good student for the art of your choice

Learn seriously and become good at it to become a Professional, who can create value to others with the art

This is a necessary step in the process of making Money

Learning takes time and effort, but you keep going

When you are ready, a Teacher for the next level appears

Meet the Real Deal

Train anything for 5-10 years, and you will be far better than any of the untrained

Yet, there are people even better in the art, the Real Deal

Meet them and learn from them

Ask them to mentor you

It is inspirational

Solve problems

If you want Money from others

You need to solve a problem for them

If the problem is big, and annoys millions of people

If the problem is serious, that calls for a high reward

You'll get bigger Money for a bigger reward

If the problem you solve is very specific

There will be someone who benefits from your solution

And they can pay Money to you

Go It Alone (Bruce Judson)
The Millionaire Fastlane (MJ DeMarco)

Do what you are good at

What you make Money from is a solution you give to others

You want to give something good

You do not make Money from what you are not good at

Focus on what you are good at

Make it even better

So you serve others far better

The works by good Professionals have one thing in common

That they are all good, far better than a layman can give

That high level of work does not come overnight

You have to work toward it

Do what counts

80% of your results come from only 20% of what you do
(The 80/20 Principle)

Focus on the 20%

Do what counts

The 80/20 Principle: The Secret to Achieving More with Less
(Richard Koch)

Right Attitude plus Specific knowledge

There are many "Success" books

Most of them teach you the right attitude toward life that helps you make Money

They can serve as a pep talk or learning aid for you

In addition, you will need industry-specific knowledge, with which you solve the problems of others

To learn the industry-specific knowledge, you need to take your time for training and apprenticeship

Even though some success may appear to come overnight,

All successful people went through learning, training and preparation in their art before their success

The Right attitude and specific knowledge, both are Important to be a successful Professional

How do you choose what you do?

Remember your past

Does it tell you something?

Why are you doing what you are doing now?

For some, it is clear. Passion guides them

For some, it's murky, but a general direction was there

For some, it's hard to determine what you would do

Ask others for help

Try testing your personality

Try testing your interests and passion

Try doing things, get hands-on experience and see you like it

Learn about yourself as you go

Career choice is a tricky issue in life. Take your time

Do What You Are: Discover the Perfect Career for You Through the Secrets of Personality Type
(Paul D. Tieger, Barbara Barron-Tieger)
Brazen Careerist (Penelope trunk)
Business model you (Timothy Clark, Alexander Osterwalder and Yves Pigneur)

Research then Commitment

You seek what you do well and are good at

Choosing it can be tricky

On the other hand you got to eat, you have your spending

You may want an easy and quick answer

But do you really want an easy and quick answer by someone else for such an important question in your life?

There is a time you do research about new things with reading, watching and doing

There is a time you make commitment to one or two things that you focus on, so you get more from the art

Devotion to an art is a two-way street

The more you give, the more you get

Track, path and Pyramid

Some professions you choose have a better-defined path to follow

You have to go to medical school to be a medical doctor
You have to go to graduate school to be a PhD
To be a nurse you have to go to the nurse's school
Specific time and training efforts have to be invested

For these professions, once you choose your path, you have to follow it through until you become the professional

Schools have a hierarchy, like a Pyramid
You can go to a top school then come down
The other way around is more difficult

Knowing these can make your career development easier

"What do you do for a living?"....Keep it simple

"What do you do for a living?"

It's a common question for adults

They ask the question

Because the answer tells an important part of who you are

To answer the question

You want to keep it simple

They usually are not asking details. Tell it within 30 seconds.

If the answer finds a place in their brain straightforwardly

That is a good answer

The art of mingling (Jeanne Martinet)

Good idea...can YOU do it?

There are good ideas that can serve others and you well

Whether YOU can realize them or not is entirely different matter

Only the completed job counts

If YOU cannot complete the good idea

The idea may not be for YOU

You either find ways to realize the good idea

Or choose another good idea that you can realize

Go It Alone (Bruce Judson)
The Success Principles (Jack Canfield)

Employer vs Employee

When you make Money for what you do,

You are a Professional

There are two types of Professionals

They are

The Employer, who hires other people to get the job done

And

The Employee, who is hired to get the job done

Both are important. Both can be rich, poor, or in between

If you want to be Very Rich, you want to become an Employer

Guide to Investing (Robert Kiyosaki)

Risk

Things do not always go as we plan or hope

There is always a Risk that things do not go well and you lose what you put in it, including Money

You decide how much Risk you want to or can take

Good business owners are very keen to minimize the Risk they take,

But they do take a calculated Risk

Risk will always be there

Learn how to handle it

"Feel Fear and Do It Anyway"

Fear is an emotion that can paralyze you to inaction

Do not let Fear take over you

Fear can be always there

It is not easy to overcome fear

You may always feel it

But Feel Fear and Do It Anyway

What counts is your action, what you do

What you feel about it has little effect on the result

Feel Fear and Do It Anyway (Susan Jeffers)

Failure is an inevitable process of the game

Making Money is a game in life

No one is good at a game from the beginning

Even if you do not want to play the game

The Game of Money is a part of this life

You must play it

In the Game, you can fail, and you will fail

Don't be afraid of failing, learn from it

Play it like an amateur, never learning how to play it

Or play it like a Pro, after learning how to play through failures

Choice is yours

Failing Forward (John Maxwell)

School can give you a protected time to learn skills to make money

Why do you want to go to school?

School can give you training, skills, knowledge and connections

They help you serve others better

It can eventually help you make Money

Education is an investment

Investments do not always return

Going to school can be wasted, if you do not learn

Aim for "Deep learning and knowledge"

What the Best College Students do (Ken Bain)
What the Best College Teachers do (Ken Bain)

Personal Branding…….

"I am X and I do Y"

You want to be useful to others

Then you have to be remembered by them to be useful to them

They want someone or something that can do the exact job

It is hard to remember someone who does not stand out

It is hard to use a tool for an unspecified purpose

As a Professional, you have to be very clear about

Who you are

What you do

To whom you serve, and

Why you do what you do

BrandSimple (Allen Adamson)
The 22 Immutable Laws of Branding (Al Ries)
Build a Brand in 30 days (Simon Middleton)
Branding Basics for Small Business (Maria Ross)

Don't be insane, but...

"If you do the same thing and expect the results to be different,

You are insane" (Albert Einstein)

If you don't like what you are getting,

You have to change what you are doing

But you need to think of balance, too

You need to be persistent to get through the process and get your result

How do you know you are just insane, or about to get your result?

This is a tough question

Talk with yourself honestly, then with others

Your passion, and how good you are, may be the key to decide

(5-2) Professionals 1: Employees

Most people make Money as an employee

Even if you want to be an Employer,

You'll need your industry-specific knowledge, and working as an employee is a great way to get the training and knowledge

Being employed is an excellent way to start off your work and Money-making

Virtue in the life of Service

You serve others

You solve problems

You do it when someone hires you to do it

That someone who hires you (your Employer) will pay you Money

In this case, you are an Employee (The Employed)

Working as an Employee is a very common way to make Money

You directly use your special skills and usefulness to your customer, to your employer, or to your co-workers

There are many ways to work as an Employee

An Employee can be expensive

Employers offer benefits to the Employees

They can include Medical Insurance, Dental Insurance, Vision Insurance, Retirement Savings (called 401k or 403b) and Matchup, paid leave etc

For the benefits, the Employer is paying Money

The total cost of hiring an Employee is much more than what an Employee sees as their paycheck

With Salary and benefits, "People" are one of the most expensive components in a company

That is why companies take hiring seriously

With own dedicated department: Human Resources, they try their best to choose the right employee

The HR Answer Book (Shawn Smith, Rebecca Mazin)

Hiring people (Employers) want to hire decent Employees

Employers hire Employees for a reason

They have a job, and they want the job done

If you, as an Employee, get the job done and done well,

Your Employer will like you

You are more valuable to your Employer

When you keep doing good work,

You are a decent and valuable Employee

Your Employer will take good care of you

Aim for it

No BS Ruthless Management (Dan Kennedy)

Be prepared and be useful

There are many different kinds of jobs

Some can be done with little training

Other jobs can be very specific and need training

Some schooling and work training are to develop people with such skills

If you are well trained, prepared, and useful, you can make a decent Employee

Employers are looking for a decent Employee

You have a better chance to get hired and make Money

Sweaty Palms (Anthony Medley)
You Inc. The Art of Selling Yourself (Harry Beckwith, Christine Clifford)
Sell yourself! Master the job interview process (Jane Williams)

Urgent vs Important

At first you may be doing what is told

Later, you will be doing things with your discretion

When you work, you have to decide what to do first, second, third….

It's called Prioritization

There are four kinds of tasks:

(1). Urgent and Important

(2). Urgent and Not Important

(3). Not urgent and Important

(4). Not urgent and Not Important

Make sure you do them from (1) to (4) in the order

Remember to do (3).

Your future depends on it

From Do It Yourself (DIY) to Teamwork

Now you have something you are good at

Someone else has something he/she is good at

Combining the two, you can do more

There will be a time you are going to think about combining what you can with what someone else can

It is the Team work

It is a major transition from DIY

When you see your Professional work as a team sport, you have better chance to do much more, and better chance to make more Money

Life in a corporate culture

Working in a big company can be an interesting experience

A big company is a collection of big teams

It gets many jobs done with many teams

Each team has a set of unique jobs

Like organs in the human body,

They support each other, doing their own jobs

Usually they have developed and have their particular ways of getting the jobs done

It's called Corporate Culture

It's helpful to know the culture in your workplace

"Mind your Surroundings"

Power: Why Some People Have It and Others Don't
(Jeffrey Pfeffer)
How to think like a CEO (DA Benton)

(5-3) Professionals 2: Employers (including the Self-Employed)

To be an employer, you have to know your business really well

If you don't know what you are doing, you are doomed

Also the life of Service, in a different manner

The Employer also has a job to be done

To get the job done, the Employer hires people and asks for their help

The Employer creates the Employee's jobs

The Employer provides services or products for the Customer

that solve the customer's problems

The Employer has more responsibility

Even when an Employee is providing the service or product

The Employer is accountable

Employer is not always a person. It can be an organization or a legal entity

Some are created to reduce the direct liability to the hiring people and to protect them

American system favors Employers

Choosing your Niche

When you want to be an Employee

You need to get the skills to get the particular job done

When you want to be an Employer

You need to decide what you provide to your Customers, who pay you Money

As an Employer, you choose where you work, and what kind of service or products you provide

Your Customer chooses your service or products, and your service or products also choose your Customer

The particular place you are in and business you do are called your Niche

Building his own business (Entrepreneur)

An Entrepreneur is a person who starts and builds his/her own business

It is not for everybody

There are particular types of people who are more adept at being an Entrepreneur

Are you one of them?

Know yourself

End of the day, results are the only thing people see

The Art of the Start (Guy Kawasaki)
My Start Up Life (Ben Casnocha)
Entrepreneur's Notebook (Steven Gold)
Start Your Own Business (Rieva Lesonsky)
Startup! (Kevin Schehrer)

The first Chip…. Get your Capital Money

Starting your own Business is an Investment

It will cost you Money and effort

Have a plan to get the Money

Save up for yourself as an Employee

Develop trust with Bankers and Investors

Build relationships with people who can help you

Other people won't give you their Money if you are broke or don't have a promising plan

To bet in a casino, you need the first Chip. It's like that

How you get the first Chip is something you need to learn or come up with yourself

Business Model

Write down the basic idea of how your business makes Money

What value do you provide?

What do you sell?

Who is your Customer?

How do you charge and collect Money?

The description is called a Business Model

Work on it

If the Model does not look promising, that means your Business is not promising, and other people are unlikely to give you their Money

Sink or Swim

When someone starts and builds a business as an Employer, as an Entrepreneur, or as a Boss,

The Single most Important Question is,

"Does the Business make Money enough to keep going?"

If not, it's a hobby or a liability

To make Money, what you provide has to appeal to the Customers

"Does what you do appeal to the Customers enough to keep going?"

Your Business sinks or swims

And you have to be responsible for it

No excuses

Great power comes with great responsibility

Working as an Employer is different from working as an Employee

As an Employer, you are responsible for your Customers and your Employees

When your Business sinks, it's on the Employer, or the Boss,

That is, on YOU

Usually the Employer, or the Boss, has more Power over the Business than the Employee

Great power comes with great responsibility

Spider-man (movie)

Think in numbers

Money is numbers

How well your Business is doing is indicated by numbers

There are specific key numbers in a specific business

Like how many cups of your lemonade sold, how much it cost you to make the lemonade, and how much Money you made

Know the key numbers for your Business and work on them

The Ten Day MBA (Steven A. Silbiger)
Go it Alone (Bruce Judson)
Street Smarts (Norm Brodsky, Bo Burlingham)

You need to work on your business, not in your business

When you are building and starting your Business,

You will be busy

But you have to have the eye of an outsider for your Business

You need to work on your Business

A Business owner is three people-in-one

An Entrepreneur, deals with the future

A Manager, deals with the past

A Technician, deals with the present

Keep your cool head and bring balance to them

The E-myth revisited (Michael Gerber)
Street Smarts (Norm Brodsky, Bo Burlingham)

Does it Work?

When you work on your Business, you have to keep asking,

"Does it work?"

If you try something new, you have to conclude, after a deadline you set, whether it worked or not

It worked when your customers saw the value

This should be indicated by an indicating number

If it worked, Continue (or improve)

If not, stop. Fix it and try something else again

Constantly evaluating whether it is working or not is the most important part of "Working on your Business"

Who/What is your Business?

Your Business should have a clear identity

Just like on page 120 [Personal Branding….. "I am X and I do Y"]

Your Business has to be very clear about

Who/What it is

What it does or sells

To whom it serves, and

Why it does/sells what it does/sells

What makes it special or unique

And keep these simple

BrandSimple (Allen Adamson)
The 22 Immutable Laws of Branding (Al Ries)
Build a Brand in 30 days (Simon Middleton)
Branding Basics for Small Business (Maria Ross)

Money is blood to your business

When the Money your Business has runs out

Or when the Money for your Business stops coming,

Your Business cannot pay its expenses

And Your Business dies

Just like we need blood to be circulating in our body

Your Business needs Money to be circulated

Money is essential for a Business to survive

Business owners build Money savings and hang on to it

Street Smarts (Norm Brodsky, Bo Burlingham)

Speed counts

Good enough is good enough. We'll fix it later

Only the completed job counts

You have to finish your preparations and get it done by the deadline

Get the feedback. If there is something to fix, fix it.

Then send it back to the market

That way you can be faster

Deadlines get the job done. An open-ended job never gets done

When you have a job to do, always ask about the deadline

The Art of the Start (Guy Kawasaki)
It's Not the Big That Eat the Small...It's the Fast That Eat the Slow
(Jason Jennings, Laurence Haughton)

Can the business sustain itself?

There is a stage when your Business makes enough Money to sustain itself

Before this stage, You have to work hard for and on the Business

After the stage, Your workload can be reduced (optional)

Build a Business that (eventually) does not need you

If you build a successful Business that does not need you,

You have the option to automate the operation

Your Business may even be manualized and franchised

Like McDonalds, KFC, Pizza Hut and IHOP

Your Business can be everywhere

That kind of Business can make a lot of Money and make you Very Rich

The E-myth revisited (Michael Gerber)

When it works, Repeat it

When you find something that works for your Business,

Repeat it

The "it" will be your main Business, until it stops working

On the other hand, you will always need to try to find something that works

It's not easy to find something that works

Find the next "it" while you still have something that works in your hands

Chapter 6: Go for the Big Money

There are Very Rich people in America

They are Very Rich because they did something that made them Very Rich

What are the "somethings"?

Money is unlimited when you know how to tap it

Very Rich people think alike, and

They tend to believe Money is unlimited, like Ocean water

Your mental image is extremely important

Just like Athletes imagine their best performance, and never imagine their poor performance,

Rich people have their performance and Money in their minds as an image

How Rich people think (Steve Siebold)
No BS Wealth Attraction (Dan Kennedy)
You were born Rich (Bob Proctor)

Who are the Very Rich people?

Self-made:

Successful Inventors

Successful Authors

Highly-paid Professionals

Celebrities

Successful Business owners

Most of them are Employers and Self-Employed

Employees can be very Rich if they have very special skills in very high demand (like a Professional football player)

Non-self-made:

Inherited/Family Rich (Silver Spoon)

Windfall Rich (Lottery winners) [Rare]

Examples of the Very Rich

- Bill Gates (Microsoft)

- Mark Zuckerberg (Facebook)

- Donald Trump (Real Estate)

- J.K. Rowling (Author of "Harry Potter" series)

- Kobe Bryant (Professional Basketball player)

Note: they don't necessarily have to be famous to be rich.

Many business builders/owners are unknown to the mass (only their Business brand).

What do they do?

Five common characteristics of Very Rich people's businesses

"NECST"

With high need ("**N**eed")

Not very easy to start up ("**E**ntry")

He has full control over ("**C**ontrol")

Impacts millions ("**S**cale")

Makes money when he sleeps ("**T**ime")

The Millionaire Fastlane (MJ DeMarco)

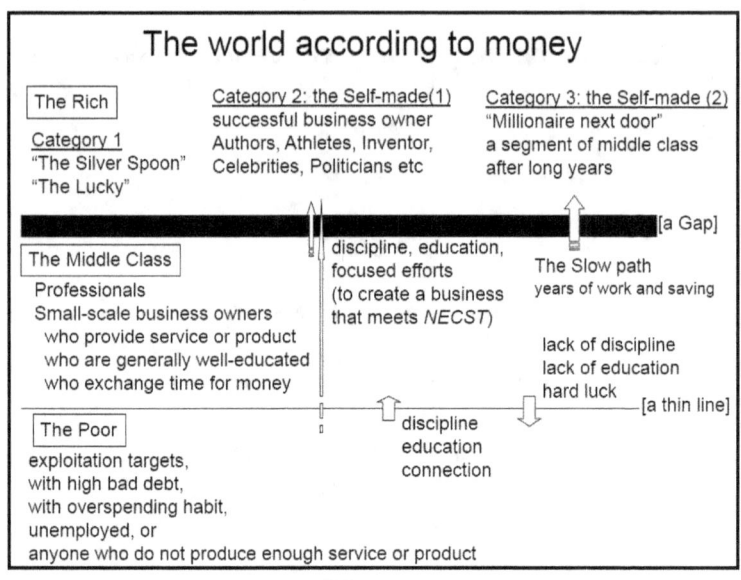

Age has little to do with being Rich

When you do something with "NECST" (page 145),

You can be Very Rich at a young age

There are many High-paying Professionals, who worked hard over the years and accumulated Money

They are Rich, and Old

It took time for them to accumulate their Money

This is why some people believe "You have to be old to be rich"

But the belief is not true

Your Choice and What you do matter

Fame, publicity and being Rich

Fame and publicity can help with being Rich in many industries

However, you do not have to be famous to be Rich

Many names of the owners of successful business are unknown to the public

Perhaps only the Brand name is known

For some celebrities whose fame counts as the source of Money (singers, actors, authors, TV personalities), no publicity is bad publicity

Observe what they do for publicity

The 48 Laws of Power (Robert Greene)

Rich people (tend to) deal only with other Rich people

By nature, Like it or not,

People are segregating

They like and look for others like them

("Birds of a feather flock together")

Rich people think alike

They went through similar processes and hardships before success and Money

They develop camaraderie, the Rich club membership

They think the club membership must be earned

"Why nibble bones when you can eat meat?"

No BS Marketing to the Affluent (Dan Kennedy)

Other People's Money

When You are Rich on your own

You have advantages over the Poor

You have proven what you are worth

You have proven you can be trusted

Other Professional people with Money, like Investors and Bankers, feel safer lending you their Money

They do not like losing their Money

They are Businesses themselves

They seek someone who can provide more Money to them

When You are Rich, it's easier to use other people's Money

You can control more Money than you actually have

Your Money and trust from others allows you to use the Leverage, control over more Money

Guide to Investing (Robert Kiyosaki)

Bring something to the table

You got to bring something to the table

Prove Your Worth and Value, have something they want, then they will come to you

Attract them, Do not chase them

Relationships tend to fall apart when both parties bring an unequal amount of something to the table

The Game (Neil Strauss)
Rules of the Game (Neil Strauss)
How to Make Anyone Fall in love with you (Leil Lowndes)
Shark Tank (TV show)

Think Win-Win

In negotiations and making deals, think win-win

Convince the other side they are getting more than they expected

The Seven Habits of highly effective people (Stephen Covey)
The Art of the Deal (Donald Trump)
Trump Style Negotiation (George Ross)

Becoming High Rollers in the Casino

Becoming Rich is similar to Becoming High Rollers in a casino

There are special tables for them
A lot of Money is dealt there

The High roller table is not another end of one table
It is a different table

To join the table, You have to bring something

You have to show your Money, and often have to have someone who can introduce you

There are many different tables in the Game of Money

Even the rules of the Game may be different at a different table

Know your table and the Game you are in

Size matters….It's a different Game Now

When you have a lot of Money,
Your Game of Money in Life is not the same as when you are with small amount of Money

You have to know this to change how you play the Game according to the size of the Money you have

When you are Rich or Wealthy, in top 10-20%,
You will have to change the way you play the Game of Money

Chapter 7: Life Long Strategy for Money

You don't know when your time ends, and your life can be longer than you think

You can make plans for your Money, so you don't outlive your Money

Be prepared to move on

Your job as an employee is not guaranteed for life

American small Companies live only for 5-10 years on average

An Exit Strategy, or plans for moving on, is important

Have one if you don't

When you build your Business, selling it is an option as your exit

The Dark Knight Rises (movie)
The Exit Strategy Handbook (Jelly Mills)

On Windfall (Lottery, Inheritance)

You can buy a lottery ticket

Or wait for a Rich relative to pass

It's okay to buy a Lottery ticket

Just don't count on it

The chance is so small, and you are not in control

Windfall is God's business

Focus on something you can control

Focus on something you can work toward

Which Quarter are you in?

A Football game has four quarters

Imagine that the Game of Money in Life has four quarters

Age 0-24: (Pre-Game. Team building, training and preparation)

Age 25-35: 1st Quarter

Age 35-45: 2nd Quarter

(Half Time)

Age 45-55: 3rd Quarter

Age 55-65: 4th Quarter

66+ (Overtime)

Where are you? Is the Game going as you planned?

Who took my Money? (Robert Kiyosaki)

Strategy and Game plan

When a Boxer with weak endurance fights, he may want to end the match early

You can make your game plan according to who you are

There are predictable paths

There are unpredictable paths

You want to learn about your chosen path as much as possible

"I worked for an Investment bank until 32. I developed my contacts and saved up some money by then. With the saving and clients, I started my company"

Some paths are not meant to last for life, like professional Athletes

They need to plan their second and later lives, while they are still active

Hajime no Ippo [Fighting Spirit] (George Morikawa)

Once you have Money

When you have Money, you want to know how to keep it, protect it, and how to have it work in your favor

Most information in the mass-media is for the middle class

You need to learn Wealth Management for the Rich

When you are Rich, you need to work with a team specialized for the Big Money (Accountant, Asset Protect Attorney, Estate Planning Attorney, Tax Attorney, Insurance Professional, Investment Advisor, Financial Planner)

Protection from loss (tax and lawsuit) becomes important

Rich people use leverage, Money and Assets, to make more Money, dealing with other Rich people

When you are Rich, the conventional idea about Money (a social reward) may not be directly applicable anymore

It is a different Game

Wealth Secrets of the Affluent (Christopher Jarvis)

There are important things other than Money

A Business makes a financial report every 3-6 months

Average American small companies live only for 5-10 years

It takes 25 years for a baby to be a man

It takes 50 years to grow a tree

Some things, once destroyed, will never come back

If you measure everything with the lifespan of Money and Business,

You will miss out on other important things that live longer

You can plan on your funeral

You can write a will

You cannot bring your Money to your afterlife

Money is good only in this world

A Legacy is about what you did, not the amount of the Money you left when you left here

Chapter 8: Grain of Salt

"Do not believe in anything simply because you have heard it.

Do not believe in anything simply because it is spoken and rumored by many.

Do not believe in anything simply because it is found written in your religious books.

Do not believe in anything merely on the authority of your teachers and elders.

Do not believe in traditions because they have been handed down for many generations.

But after observation and analysis, when you find that anything agrees with reason and is conducive to the good and benefit of one and all, then accept it and live up to it"

Buddha

Everyone speaks for himself

Everyone speaks for himself from his/her own standpoint, so there are many opinions

Not all opinions work equally well

You have to distinguish opinions that work well for you, and opinions that are harmful to you

When someone speaks his/her opinion about Money,

The person can speak about what worked for him/her

But they cannot say whether it will work for you

People do what works for them

Search Good Professionals for your Money Team, but get second opinion like it is a Medical team

The Six Figure Second Income (David Lindahl, Jonathan Rozek)
Life Strategies (Philip Mcgraw [aka Dr. Phil])

Conflict of Interests may not be mentioned

You have your own interest

They have their own interests

When these are aligned well, you can create a Win-Win situation

What if these interests are not well aligned, or are even conflicted?

That can result in a Win-Lose, or a Lose-Lose situation

Consider this possibility

The Little Book of Common Sense Investing (John Bogle)
Take on the Street (Arthur Levitt)
The Only Guide to a Winning Investment Strategy You'll Ever Need (Larry Swedroe)

Who is speaking?

When it comes to make Money, would you rather listen to your Rich uncle, or your Poor uncle?

When you hear information,

You need to check the source of information, or who is speaking

How well the source is doing in the subject is an important thing to consider

"We talk about a batting rate for baseball players. Somehow we don't talk about how rich those financial advisers are, how they make their Money"

When you are Rich, you ask other Rich people to refer good Professionals who can serve you well

These are qualified Professionals who can get the job done for you, and their opinions matter

Be Educated

Continue learning and working on your Money

By choosing what you do, you choose how much you make

By choosing how you manage your Money, you choose how much you keep

You and your Money are in a lifelong relationship

What will you learn in next 5 years?

Who will you meet in next 5 years?

What will you do in next 5 years?

They will determine the Money you will make 5 years later

You have many choices to make

Keep educating yourself and make wise choices

Further Learning Suggestions

(Alphabetical by the title)

Materials referred in the text

22 Immutable Laws of Branding, The (Al Ries)
80/20 Principle: The Secret to Achieving More with Less, The (Richard Koch)
48 Laws of Power, The (Robert Greene)
$100 Startup, The (Chris Guillebeau)
177 Mental Toughness Secrets of the World Class (Steve Siebold)
Aesop's Fables
Aladdin Factor, The (Jack Canfield, Mark Victor Hansen)
Art of the Deal, The (Donald Trump)
Art of mingling, The (Jeanne Martinet)
Art of the Start, The (Guy Kawasaki)
Auto Repair for Dummies (Deanna Sclar)
Bible, The
Branding Basics for Small Business (Maria Ross)
BrandSimple (Allen Adamson)
Brazen Careerist (Penelope trunk)
Buddhist proverb
Build a Brand in 30 days (Simon Middleton)
Business Model You (Timothy Clark, Alexander Osterwalder and Yves Pigneur)
Cashvertising (Drew Eric Whitman)
Dark Knight Rises, The (*movie*)
Details Men's Style Manual (Daniel Peres)
Devil wears Prada, The (*movie*)
Do More Great Work (Michael Bungay Stainer, et al.)
Do What You Are: Discover the Perfect Career for You Through the Secrets of Personality Type (Paul D. Tieger, Barbara Barron-Tieger)
Essays of Warren Buffett: Lessons for Corporate America, The (Warren Buffet, Laurence Cunningham)
E-myth revisited, The (Michael Gerber)
Entrepreneur's Notebook (Steven Gold)
Exit Strategy Handbook, The (Jelly Mills)

Failing Forward (John Maxwell)
Feel Fear and Do It Anyway (Susan Jeffers)
Feng Shui Your Life (Jayme Barrett)
Game, The (Neil Strauss)
Gentleman's Guide to Grooming and Style (Bernhard Roetzel)
Go It Alone (Bruce Judson)
Good Fight, The (Les&Leslie Parrott)
Green Pharmacy Guide to Healing Foods, The (James Duke)
Guide to Investing (Robert Kiyosaki)
Hajime no Ippo [Fighting Spirit] (George Morikawa)
Home Buying for Dummies (Eric Tyson, Ray Brown)
How to Make Anyone Fall in love with you (Leil Lowndes)
How to think like a CEO (DA Benton)
How Rich People Think (Steve Siebold)
HR Answer Book, The (Shawn Smith, Rebecca Mazin)
I Could Do Anything If I Only Knew What It Was (Barbara Sher, Barbara Smith)
It's Not the Big That Eat the Small...It's the Fast That Eat the Slow (Jason Jennings, Laurence Haughton)
Law of Attraction (Michael Losier)
Life Strategies (Philip Mcgraw [Dr. Phil])
Little Book of Common Sense Investing, The (John Bogle)
Magic of Thinking Big, The (David Schwartz)
Making Ideas Happen (Scott Belsky)
Making a Living Without a Job, revised edition (Barbara Winter)
Millionaire Fastlane, The (MJ DeMarco)
Millionaire Next Door, The (Thomas Stanley, William Danko)
Money Book for Young, Fabulous and Broke, The (Suze Orman)
Multiple Streams of Income (Robert G. Allen)
My Start Up Life (Ben Casnocha)
Mythbusters (*TV show*)
No BS marketing to the Affluent (Dan Kennedy)
No BS Ruthless Management (Dan Kennedy)
No BS Wealth Attraction (Dan Kennedy)
Ogilvy on Advertising (David Ogilvy)
Only Guide to a Winning Investment Strategy You'll Ever Need, The (Larry Swedroe)
Pocket Stylist, The (Kendall Farr)

Power: Why Some People Have It and Others Don't (Jeffrey Pfeffer)
Real Age Diet, the (Michael Roizen, John La Puma)
Rich Dad Poor Dad (Robert Kiyosaki)
Richest Man in Babylon, The (George S. Clason)
Rules of the Game (Neil Strauss)
Sartorialist, The (Scott Schuman)
Secret, The (Rhonda Byrne)
Secrets of the Millionaire Mind (T. Harv Eker)
Sell yourself! Master the job interview process (Jane Williams)
Seven Habits of Highly Effective People, The (Stephen Covey)
Shark Tank (*TV show*)
Six Figure Second Income, The (David Lindahl, Jonathan Rozek)
Spider-man (*movie*)
Startup! (Kevin Schehrer)
Start Your Own Business (Rieva Lesonsky)
Street Smarts (Norm Brodsky, Bo Burlingham)
Success Principles, The (Jack Canfield)
Suze Orman Show, The (*TV show*)
Sweaty Palms (Anthony Medley)
Take on the Street (Arthur Levitt)
Ten Day MBA 4th Ed., The (Steven A. Silbiger)
Tested Advertising Methods (John Caples)
Thoughts are Things (Napoleon Hill)
Trump Style Negotiation (George Ross)
You are born Rich (Bob Proctor)
You Inc. The Art of Selling Yourself (Harry Beckwith, Christine Clifford)
Wealth Secrets of the Affluent (Christopher Jarvis)
What the Best College Students do (Ken Bain)
What the Best College Teachers do (Ken Bain)
Who took my Money? (Robert Kiyosaki)
Ultimate Suburban Survivalist Guide, The (Sean Brodrick)

Additional Materials consulted for this book

33 Strategies of War, The (Robert Greene)
Art of SpeedReading People, The (Paul D. Tieger, Barbara Barron-Tieger)
Art of War, The (Sun Tzu)
Beating the Street (Peter Lynch)
Business Communication (Mary Ellen Guffey, Dana Loewy)
Clark Howard (*TV show*)
Coaching Mental Toughness (Steve Siebold)
Complete Works of Florence Scovel Shinn, The (Florence Scovel Shinn)
Dramatic Success (Andrew Leigh, Michael Maynard)
Essential Drucker (Peter Drucker)
First Impressions (Ann Demarais Ph.D. and Valerie White)
Five Temptations of a CEO, The (Patrick Lencioni)
Getting loaded (Peter Bielagus)
Getting Results the Agile Way (J.D. Meier, Michael Kropp)
Good to Great (Jim Collins)
Hard Optimism (Price Pritchett)
How I made my Millions (*TV show*)
How to Resolve Conflicts at Work (Florence M. Stone)
Influence (Robert Cialdini)
Instant Persuasion (Laurie Puhn)
Investment Fables (Aswath Damodaran)
Leadership and Self-deception (Arbinger Institute)
Lean Startup, The (Eric Ries)
Left-Brain Finance for Right-Brain People (Paula Ann Monroe)
Life Lessons for Mastering the Law of Attraction (Jack Canfield, et al.)
Life's missing instruction manual (Joe Vitale)
Low Stress Investing (Andrew Millard)
Made to stick (Chip Heath, Dan Heath)
Master Key System, The (Charles F. Haanel)
Mastery (Robert Greene)
Matrix, The (*movie*)
Maximize your potential (The 99U book series)
Millionaire Messenger, The (Brendon Burchard)
Morningstar Guide to Mutual Funds (Christine Benz)
No BS grassroots marketing (Dan Kennedy)
Personal Finance for Busy People (Robert A Cooke)
Personal Finance for Dummies (Eric Tyson)

Real Money (Jim Cramer)
Rules For Revolutionaries (Guy Kawasaki, Michele Moreno)
Secret of the Ages (Robert Collier)
Science of getting rich, The (Wallace D. Wattles)
Science of Success, The (James Arthur Ray)
So Good they can't ignore you (Cal Newport)
Someone Will Make Money on Your Funds - Why Not You (Gary Gastineau)
Speak like a CEO (Suzanne Bates)
Talent Code, The (Daniel Coyle)
Talent is overrated (Geoff Colvin)
Talent is never enough (John C. Maxwell)
Ten Roads to Riches, The (Ken Fischer)
Thinker's Toolkit, The (Morgan D. Jones)
Will It Sell? How to Determine If Your Invention Is Profitably Marketable (James E. White)

Reader's Responses

"This is an extremely smart book"

"It's written in a poetry/how-to hybrid writing style. After reading George's book, I wondered why they had to write that much in these other books"

"Over 130 great books in one"

"I'll take this book to our family trip"

"There are many short, Zen-style Money questions in this book. But overall, it is an instruction book"

"I wish he had written this book earlier"

About the Author

George N. Yamagata is a son of an immigrant. George is a researcher (professional scientist with a PhD) in his 40s. He lives with his wife, two children and a cat. Facing the financially diverse society of America, he set off to answer a question for his children, wife, and himself, "Why and how are some people rich?"

In conclusion, George says,

"We got to teach our kids about Money. And I wanted to teach good lessons for them. This book is a compilation of the Money wisdom from many other books and blogs. For this book, I worked like a curator in the museum, and it was very enjoyable process.

I wanted this book to be a practical guide for the young. It was not meant to be spiritual pep talk nor success preaching. The contents are not my personal opinions, so it doesn't matter who I am. What matters is the usefulness of the contents of this book, and how you use the contents in the Game of Money in your life. What you choose and do count. Good luck."

George can be contacted at: GeorgeYamagata@gmail.com

www.ingramcontent.com/pod-product-compliance
Lightning Source LLC
Chambersburg PA
CBHW071758200526
45167CB00017B/440